United States
Department of
Agriculture

Forest Service

Pacific Northwest
Research Station

General Technical Report
PNW-GTR-836

March 2011

Cap and Trade

Offsets and Implications for Alaska

Joseph A. Roos, Valerie Barber, and Allen M. Brackley

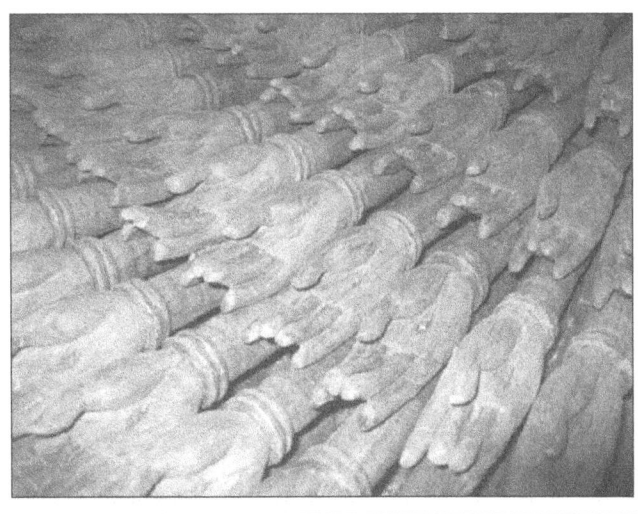

Authors

Joseph A. Roos is a research associate, University of Washington, Seattle, WA 98105; **Valerie Barber** is an assistant professor, Forest Products Program, University of Alaska-Fairbanks, Palmer, AK 99645; and **Allen M. Brackley** is a research forester, U.S. Department of Agriculture, Forest Service, Pacific Northwest Research Station, Alaska Wood Utilization Research and Development Center, 204 Siginaka Way, Sitka, AK 99835.

Cover photographs, providing examples of temporary carbon storage in products (clockwise from top left): spiritual statuary (Thousand Hand Buddha) and Starrigavin Creek Cabin, Tongass National Forest, by Allen M. Brackley; red alder lumber and sawmill company logo, by David L. Nicholls.

Abstract

Roos, Joseph A.; Barber, Valerie; Brackley, Allen M. 2011. Cap and trade: offsets and implications for Alaska. Gen. Tech. Rep. PNW-GTR-836. Portland, OR: U.S. Department of Agriculture, Forest Service, Pacific Northwest Research Station. 27 p.

The Environmental Protection Agency (EPA) has formally declared that greenhouse gases (GHG) pose a threat to public health and the environment. This is significant because it gives the executive branch the authority to impose carbon regulations on carbon-emitting entities. United States GHG emissions have increased by approximately 17 percent between 1990 and 2007, and the EPA now has the authority to design regulation to reverse this trend. One of the regulatory tools being considered is a cap and trade system, whereby a ceiling is set for allowable carbon dioxide emissions and emitters are allowed to purchase offsets if they exceed their allowable emissions. Forests are major carbon sinks, and reforestation or projects to avoid deforestation are considered an offset with a monetary value under a majority of cap and trade systems. Alaska has vast forest resources including the largest national forest in the Nation. Alaska's forest accounts for 17 percent of all U.S. forest land. This paper provides an overview of a cap and trade system, the role of offsets, and the potential impact on Alaska's forest stakeholders.

Keywords: Forests, carbon, carbon trading offsets, Alaska, climate change.

Introduction

On April 17, 2009, the Environmental Protection Agency (EPA) formally announced that it had found that greenhouse gas (GHG) poses a threat to public health and the environment (EPA 2009a). This announcement was significant because it gives the executive branch the authority to impose carbon regulations on carbon-emitting entities. United States GHG emissions have increased by approximately 17 percent between 1990 and 2007, and the EPA now has the authority to design regulation to reverse this trend. One of the regulatory tools being considered is a cap and trade system, whereby a ceiling is set for allowable carbon dioxide (CO_2) emissions and emitters are allowed to purchase credits if they exceed their allowable emissions.

The EPA announcement brings the United States closer to participating in a global cap and trade agreement. The organization that drafts these global climate change agreements is the United Nations Framework Convention on Climate Change (UNFCCC). The first major climate change agreement developed under the UNFCCC was the Kyoto Protocol, which went into effect February 2005. The Kyoto Protocol set targets for 37 industrialized countries and the European community to reduce GHG emissions to an average of 5 percent below 1990 levels over the 5-year period from 2008 through 2012. Although the Kyoto Protocol is the first international agreement addressing GHGs, the agreement has two major limitations. First, some of the world's largest GHG emitters including China, India, and the United States, did not sign the Kyoto Protocol, which severely limits the agreement's effectiveness. Second, the agreement does not directly address tropical deforestation. Annex 1 countries (industrialized economies and economies in transition) are allowed to achieve some target emission reductions by investing in energy and tree planting projects (reforestation and afforestation) through the "Clean Development Mechanism" stipulated in the Kyoto Protocol. However, this provides little incentive for countries that are at high risk for deforestation, such as Brazil, Indonesia, Bolivia, Peru, Columbia, and central African nations to protect their tropical forests. It has been proposed that eliminating deforestation in Brazil and Indonesia during the Kyoto Protocol period would equal approximately 80 percent of emission reductions gained by the Kyoto Protocol (Santilli et al. 2005). The Kyoto Protocol is set to expire in 2012, and a new global agreement to mitigate climate change is currently being debated.

In December 2009, the United Nations held a climate change conference in Copenhagen to draft a climate change agreement to follow the Kyoto Protocol. This conference included 193 countries and resulted in a draft of an agreement called the Copenhagen Accord (UNFCCC 2009). Although the draft has not been finalized, one area the Copenhagen Accord focuses on is the United Nation's framework to reduce deforestation called Reducing Emissions from Deforestation and Forest Degradation (REDD). The strategy of REDD is to reward countries, companies, and forest-land owners for maintaining their forests rather than cutting them down, while avoiding CO_2 leakage. The REDD program relies on a trust fund, established in September 2008, that allows donors to pool resources and provides funding for activities toward this program. The core concept is that wealthier nations will contribute to the trust fund and subsidize developing nations for maintaining their forests and for increasing the carbon sink potential of their forests.

Item 6 of the Copenhagen Accord (UNFCCC 2009) reads:

> We recognize the crucial role of reducing emission from deforestation and forest degradation and the need to enhance removals of greenhouse gas emission by forests and agree on the need to provide positive incentives to such actions through the immediate establishment of a mechanism including REDD-plus, to enable the mobilization of financial resources from developed countries.

There are still many issues of disagreement among the participating countries of the Copenhagen conference. Before an agreement can be reached, a major rift needs to be closed between developed and developing countries.

As stated above, the United States did not sign onto the Kyoto Protocol. However, there are two bills discussed below that are being debated. These bills would mandate a cap and trade system in the United States. Both of these bills include provisions for forest-related offsets, and, if passed, would impact forest stakeholders throughout the United States. In summary, forest-based offsets are an important part of climate change mitigation mechanisms at the international, national, regional, and state levels, and it is important for Alaskan forest stakeholders to understand the forest's role in these mechanisms.

Greenhouse Gas Measurement

The basis for GHG emission measurement is the carbon dioxide equivalent (CO_2e). A CO_2e measures each gas by its global warming potential (GWP), which is the universal standard of measurement. A GWP is based on the ability of each GHG to trap heat in the atmosphere relative to an equivalent unit of CO_2 over a specified period of time. Table 1 shows both the GWP unit and the percentage of total GHG emissions. The table highlights the intensive GHG warming potential of sulphur hexafluoride. Although the quantity of emissions released into the atmosphere is less than 1 percent of the total, its ability to trap heat in the atmosphere is 23,900

Table 1—Global warming potential in carbon dioxide equivalents (CO_2e)

Gas category	Global warming potential	Percentage of 2007 total greenhouse gas emissions (CO_2e basis)
	CO_2e	*Percent*
Carbon dioxide	1	85
Methane	21	8
Nitrous oxide	310	4
Halocarbons (various compounds)	140 (HFC-152a) to 11,700 (HFC-23)	2
Sulphur hexafluoride	23,900	<1

HFC = hydrofluorocarbon.
HFC-152a and HFC-23 represent the range of warming potential halocarbons.
Source: EPA 2009c, IETA 2009.

times that of CO_2. Therefore, in addition to reducing emissions of CO_2, climate change mitigation policies need to reduce emissions in all the major GHG categories.

Global Emissions

In 2006, total global emissions were estimated to be 29 billion metric tons of CO_2e and are predicted to increase to 33.1 billion metric tons by 2015 (EIA 2009). The top five emitters are the United States, China, the Russian Federation, India, and Japan (table 2). These figures illustrate a major limitation of the Kyoto Protocol, which is that the world's largest emitters are not regulated by the Kyoto Protocol.

Table 2—Emissions of major emitting countries (countries with at least annual 500 million metric tons of carbon dioxide equivalents [CO_2e])

Country	CO_2e	Percentage change since 1990	CO_2e per capita
	Million metric tons	*Percent*	*Metric tons*
United States	7,017.32	14.4	22.96
China	6,103.35[a]	—	3.39[b]
Russian Federation	2,190.24	-34.2	15.37
India	1,510.35[a]	—	1.30[b]
Japan	1,340.08	5.3	10.51
Germany	1,004.79	-18.2	12.20
Canada	720.63	21.7	22.09
Brazil	658.65[a]	11.1	4.14[b]
United Kingdom	655.79	-15.1	10.83
Italy	567.92	9.9	9.63
Mexico	548.5	29.2	5.38
France	546.53	-3.5	8.90
Australia	536.07	28.8	25.99

[a] Figure reported in million metric tons of CO_2 (rather than CO_2e).
[b] Figure for reported year of 1994.
Source: United Nations Statistics Division 2009.

In addition to total emissions emitted by each country, it is important to examine per capita emissions. When the emissions are measured on a per capita basis, the top five countries are Australia, the United States, Canada, the Russian Federation, the United Kingdom, and Germany. The discrepancy in per capita emissions between developed and developing countries were the seed of major disagreements at the Copenhagen Conference.

United States Emissions

The EPA provides estimates for CO_2 emissions in the United States. The unit of measure used by the EPA is teragrams of carbon dioxide equivalents ($TgCO_2e$). According to EPA estimates, total GHG in the United States in 2007 were 7,150.1 $TgCO_2e$ (table 3).

The majority of U.S. GHG emissions are caused by fossil fuel combustion, which accounted for 80 percent of the 2007 total. The goal of the Kyoto Protocol was to reduce GHG emissions of its members by 5 percent below 1990 levels. As mentioned earlier, the United States is not bound by the Kyoto Protocol requirements, and it is interesting to note that U.S. emissions between 1990 and 2007 increased by 17 percent. The largest source of emissions in the United States is transportation, followed by the industrial, residential, and commercial sectors (fig. 1).

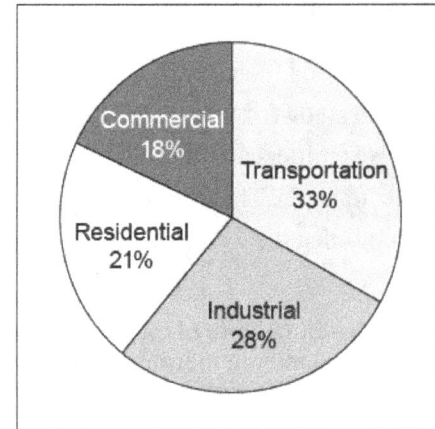

Figure 1—Percentage of U.S. emissions sources by sector. Source: EPA 2009c.

Table 3—U.S. carbon emission

Gas/source	1990	1995	2000	2005	2006	2007
	Teragrams carbon dioxide equivalents					
Carbon dioxide	5,076.7	5,407.9	5,955.2	6,090.8	6,014.9	6,103.4
Methane	616.6	615.8	591.1	561.7	582.0	585.3
Nitrous oxide	315.0	334.1	329.2	315.9	312.1	311.9
Hydrofluorocarbons	36.9	61.8	100.1	116.1	119.1	125.5
Perfluorinated compounds	20.8	15.6	13.5	6.2	6.0	7.5
Sulphur hexafluoride	32.8	28.1	19.2	17.9	17.0	16.5
Total	6,098.7	6,463.3	7,008.2	7,108.6	7,051.1	7,150.1

Source: EPA 2009c.

Transportation Sector

The transportation sector comprised 33 percent of total U.S. CO_2 emissions in 2007. Transportation emissions rose by 29 percent between 1990 and 2007. According to the EPA, this rise can be attributed to increased demand for travel and the stagnation of fuel efficiency of U.S. vehicles. The largest sources of transportation GHGs in 2007 were passenger cars (33 percent); light duty trucks, which include sport utility vehicles, pickup trucks, and minivans (28 percent); freight trucks (21 percent); and commercial aircraft (8 percent). Passenger cars and light duty trucks increased by 40 percent owing to population growth, economic growth, urban sprawl, and lower fuel prices (EPA 2009c).

Industrial Sector

The industrial sector is the second largest emitting category. In 2007, the industrial sector accounted for 28 percent of total U.S. emissions. The EPA defines the industrial sector as all manufacturing facilities plus emissions that are a byproduct of the non-energy-related industrial process activities such as fugitive[1] methane emissions (CH_4); emissions from coal mining; byproduct CO_2 emissions from cement manufacturing; and hydrofluorocarbon, perfluorinated compounds, and sulphur hexafluoride byproduct emissions from semiconductor manufacturing. Overall, industrial sector emissions have declined since 1990. This reflects a shift in the U.S. economy from heavy industries such as steel to lighter industries such as technology. Although industrial sector emissions have declined in the United States, industrial sector emissions have increased in developing countries such as China as heavy industrial production shifts from the United States to developing countries.

Residential Sector

The third category, the residential sector, made up 21 percent of total U.S. emissions in 2007. The residential sector includes all emissions arising from residential activity including HVAC (heating, ventilation, and air conditioning), cooking, and appliance use. Emissions in this category increased between 1990 and 2007, largely reflecting the increase in the U.S. population. Between 1990 and 2007, the U.S. population increased from 250 to 302 million, which was about a 20 percent increase (U.S. Census Bureau 2010).

Commercial Sector

The commercial sector contributes nonindustrial emissions that arise from commercial activities, and, in 2007, constituted (or formed) 21 percent of U.S.

---

[1] Fugitive emissions are emissions that are released through events such as leaks, spills, and evaporation.

emissions. As with the residential sector, the commercial sector is heavily reliant on electricity. A majority of emissions in this category come from electricity for lighting, heating, air conditioning, and operating appliances (EPA 2009c). This category also includes emissions from natural gas, petroleum products, landfills, and wastewater treatment facilities. Overall, this category has increased owing to a variety of factors including weather and economic activity.

U.S. Carbon Sequestration

The largest source of carbon sequestration in the United States is forests. Forests sequester approximately 910 $TgCO_2e$ annually, which is about 12 percent of annual U.S. emissions (table 4). Although forests are by far the largest category of carbon sequestration, other categories include urban trees, agricultural soil, yard trimmings, and food scraps. Another category not included in the table is harvested wood products. It was estimated that the annual sequestration of harvested wood products in 2000 was 108.5 $TgCO_2e$ (Skog 2008).

Table 5 shows the approximate correlations of U.S. gross domestic product (GDP) growth to U.S. GHG emissions from 1990 to 2007. The table shows that the annual GDP growth rate has exceeded the emissions growth rate. This may be the result of industry becoming more energy efficient. However, it can also be partially attributed to a large portion of U.S. heavy industry manufacturing such as steel moving to developing countries such as India and China. This illustrates the importance of pursuing a global agreement so that increased U.S. regulation does not act as an incentive to shift manufacturing to countries with weaker or no GHG regulations.

Table 4—Recent trends in U.S. greenhouse gas emissions and sinks

	1990	1995	2000	2005	2006	2007
	Teragrams carbon dioxide equivalents					
Total emissions	6,098.7	6,463.3	7,008.2	7,108.6	7,051.1	7,150.1
Carbon dioxide sequestration from forests	-661.1	-686.6	-512.6	-975.7	-900.3	-910.1
Carbon dioxide from urban trees	-60.6	-71.5	-82.4	-93.3	-95.5	-97.6
Carbon dioxide sequestration from agricultural soil carbon stocks	-96.3	-78.9	-111.2	-43.6	-44.5	-45.1
Carbon dioxide from landfills, yard trimmings, and food scraps	-23.5	-13.9	-11.3	-10.2	-10.4	-9.8
Total carbon dioxide in sinks	-841.4	-851	-717.5	-1,122.7	-1,050.5	-1,062.6
Total net emissions (sources and sinks)	5,257.3	5,612.3	6,290.7	5,985.9	6,000.6	6,087.5

[a] Totals may not sum owing to independent rounding.
Source: EPA 2009c.

Table 5—Correlation of gross domestic product (GDP) growth to greenhouse gas emissions (index 1990 = 100)

Variable	1990	1995	2000	2005	2006	2007	Mean growth rate	Correlation to GDP growth
			Percent					
Annual GDP growth	100	113	138	155	159	162	2.9	1
Greenhouse gas emissions	100	106	115	117	115	117	0.9	.922

Source: EPA 2009c.

Alaska's emission sources—

Alaska's 2010 GHG emissions are projected to be 53.5 million metric tons (MMT) of CO_2e and are projected to grow to 62.8 MMT CO_2e by 2025 (table 6). The major 2010 emissions sources are industrial fuel (26.5 MMT CO_2e), transportation (18.5 MMT CO_2e), residential/commercial fuel (3.91 MMT CO_2e), and electricity (3.58 MMT CO_2e). The remaining 1.9 percent of emissions is composed of agriculture, industrial processes, and waste management.

Of Alaska's total emissions, the production of industrial fuel is by far the largest source, accounting for 50 percent of the total (fig. 2). The industrial fuel category is composed of natural gas (75 percent), petroleum/oil (22 percent), and coal (3 percent). Alaska's second largest source of emissions is transportation, which makes up 34 percent of total emissions. The transportation category is composed of aviation (71 percent), on-road vehicles (25 percent), and marine vessels (4 percent). The third largest source of emissions is the residential/commercial fuel, which is slightly over 7 percent of the total (Center for Climate Strategies 2009). The residential/commercial fuel category is composed of natural gas (49 percent), petroleum/oil industry (33 percent), coal (17 percent), and wood (1 percent). Alaska's fourth largest emissions source is electricity generation, which is 7 percent of the total. This category includes natural gas (62 percent), oil (24 percent), and coal (14 percent).

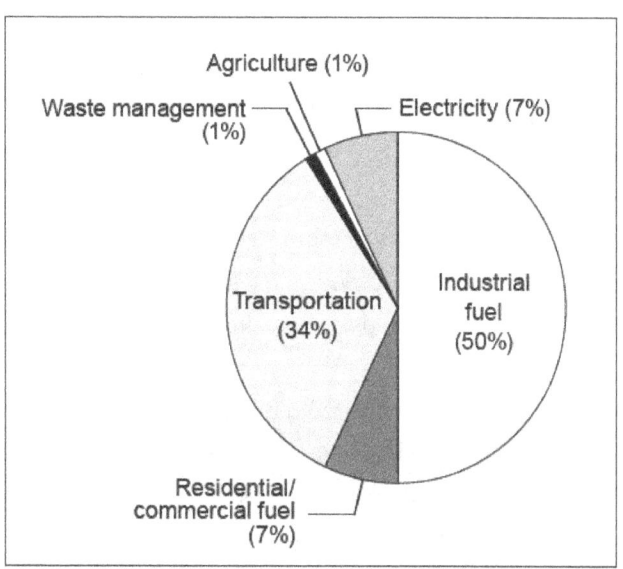

Figure 2—Alaska's emissions by category. Source: Center for Climate Strategies 2009.

Table 6—Alaska emissions

Sector	1990	2000	2005	2010	2020	2025
	Million metric tons carbon dioxide equivalents					
Electricity use (consumption):						
Coal	0.40	0.42	0.48	0.50	0.79	0.79
Natural gas	2.00	2.29	2.14	2.22	2.36	2.36
Oil	0.37	0.48	0.57	0.86	0.58	0.86
Subtotal[a]	2.76	3.19	3.20	3.58	3.74	4.02
Residential/commercial fuel use:						
Coal	0.76	0.79	0.70	0.69	0.67	0.66
Natural gas	1.79	2.22	1.87	1.91	2.09	2.13
Petroleum	1.21	1.30	1.29	1.29	1.34	1.26
Wood (CH_4 and N_2O)[b]	0.01	0.01	0.02	0.02	0.02	0.02
Subtotal[a]	3.77	4.33	3.88	3.91	4.12	4.07
Industrial fuel use/fossil fuel industry:						
Coal/coal mining	0.76	0.79	0.70	0.69	0.67	0.66
Natural gas/natural gas industry	13.40	17.70	19.10	20.50	25.10	26.10
Petroleum/oil industry	7.10	5.18	5.57	5.98	5.78	5.60
Wood (CH_4 and N_2O)[b]	0.012	0	0	0	0	0
Subtotal[a]	20.5	22.9	24.7	26.5	30.9	31.8
Transportation:						
Aviation	7.15	10.60	12.90	13.10	13.40	13.70
Marine vessels	0.83	0.48	0.61	0.72	1.00	1.17
On-road vehicles	3.41	3.71	4.19	4.55	5.57	6.20
Rail and other	0.08	0.08	0.06	0.06	0.06	0.06
Subtotal[a]	11.5	14.9	17.8	18.5	20.1	21.1
Industrial processes	0.051	0.200	0.330	0.450	0.750	0.960
Waste management	0.320	0.530	0.630	0.520	0.730	0.860
Agriculture	0.053	0.054	0.053	0.056	0.066	0.073
Total gross emissions (consumption basis)[a]	39.0	46.1	50.6	53.5	60.3	62.8

[a] Totals may not sum owing to rounding at the source.
[b] CH_4 = methane; N_2O = nitrous oxide.
Source: Center for Climate Strategies 2009.

Alaska's forest ownership structure includes the federal government, the state government, native corporations, and private ownership. Federal climate change legislation with a provision for forest-related offsets will impact each of these groups in different ways. Whether it is the Waxman-Markey Bill, the Kerry-Lieberman Bill, or EPA-mandated reductions, Alaska will be required to absorb a highly complex system regarding allowances and offsets for GHGs. Therefore, it will be important for Alaska policymakers to design a strategy to educate all stakeholders regarding climate change legislation and the impact on stakeholder operations once legislation is passed and becomes law. The next section presents an overview of cap and trade systems and how offsets are defined within these systems.

Carbon Trading and Offsets

To understand carbon trading, it is important to understand the products that are being traded. The primary product in carbon markets is the trading of GHG emission allowances. Under a cap and trade system, permits are issued to various entities for the right to emit GHG emissions that meet emission reduction requirement caps. An offset is defined as the reduction, removal, or avoidance of GHG emissions from a specific project that is then used to compensate for GHG emissions occurring elsewhere (Offset Quality Initiative 2008).

Offsets are an established component of various emission reduction programs including the Kyoto Protocol, the European Union Emissions Trading Scheme, the Regional Greenhouse Gas Initiative, and the Western Climate Initiative. One essential part of any climate change mitigation agreement is establishing strong criteria for GHG offsets. There are four criteria for including offsets in a climate change mitigation program. The avoidance or removal of a GHG must be real, additional, verifiable, and permanent (WCI 2009). The criterion of "real" assures that the offset results in an actual avoidance or removal of GHGs rather than a project that does not produce actual results beneficial to the environment. The criterion of "additional" assures that the offset reduces or avoids emissions more than a baseline scenario without the project. Furthermore, the offset must be created for the specific purpose of GHG removal or avoidance rather than a project that would have occurred anyway. The criterion of "verifiable" assures that the offsets can be verified by an independent third-party organization. Finally, the criterion of "permanence" assures that a minimum time requirement for the longevity of the offset is included and that there is no leakage. Leakage is when deforestation is avoided in one region at the expense of increased deforestation of another region (Brown 2002). There are various offset mechanisms to accommodate different kinds of GHG reduction programs (table 7).

An example of an organization addressing forest-related offsets is the Climatic Action Reserve. This organization was founded to ensure the integrity, transparency, and financial value in the North American carbon market. Eligibility rules and requirements under the Forest Project Protocol prepared by the Climatic Action Reserve are outlined in a draft submitted in July 2009 (CAR 2009). The draft addresses requirements for offsets including additionality, project start date, crediting period, minimum time commitment, implementation agreement, easements to insure continuation in the event of change of ownership, attestation of title, location of project, and sustainability of applied practices.

Table 7—Examples of offset mechanisms, regulations, and verification organizations

Alberta-Based Offset Credit System	Created for entities regulated under Alberta's mandatory greenhouse gas (GHG) emission regulations. Established protocols were created by the Alberta government in conjunction with stakeholders, defining offset requirements. Forestry-based offsets are currently under review.
British Columbia Emission Offset Regulation	Created for British Columbia's (BC) Greenhouse Gas Reduction Target Act of 2008 This legislation set the goal to reduce emissions to 33 percent below 2007 levels by 2020. Forest-based offsets are included and regulated by BC Forest Offset Protocol.
California Global Warming Solutions Act of 2006	Established an emissions reduction program to reduce emissions to 1990 levels by 2020. The GHG emissions reduction program will begin being implemented in 2011. Forest offsets are allowed for afforestation, improved forest management, and avoided conversion of forest land.
Protocol Clean Development Mechanism (CDM)	Established under the Protocol and allows a country with an emission-reduction or emission-limitation commitment under the Protocol (Annex B Party) to implement an emission-reduction project in developing countries. Forest offsets are included for afforestation and reforestation.
Protocol Joint Implementation (JI)	This offset mechanism was also developed under the Protocol and allows a country with an emission reduction or limitation commitment under the Protocol (Annex B Party) to earn Emission Reduction Units from an emission-reduction or mission removal project in another Annex B Party country. Forest-based offsets are allowed as described with clean development mechanism (CDM).
International Organization for Standardization (ISO 14064)	The ISO 14064 standards for GHG accounting and verification were launched in 2006. This offset verification system provides government and industry with a transparent system to account for the reduction and trading of GHG emissions. This provides a standard to account for forestry-based offsets.
Regional Greenhouse Gas Initiative (RGGI)	RGGI set up an offset system that is project based. It includes project categories that can be used to offset compliance five obligations of member states. Forest-based offsets are allowed for afforestation.
Gold Standard	This is a voluntary carbon offset standard developed by the World Wildlife Fund for renewable energy and energy efficiency projects. Forest-based offsets are verified to assure their compliance with CDM and Joint Implementation regulations.
Voluntary Carbon Standard	This standard was established to verify the validity of reductions and removals of carbon by offset projects. Forest based-offsets are verified for afforestation and reforestation projects.

Source: WCI 2009.

Forestry-Based Offsets

There are four general types of forestry-based offset projects: afforestation, reforestation, reduced deforestation, and harvested wood products. Forestry-based offsets fall under the Land Use and Land-Use Change and Forestry section under the Kyoto Protocol. One of the main drawbacks of these forestry-based offsets is that the carbon sequestered may be reversed and re-released into the atmosphere (Perez-Garcia and Lippke 2008). This can happen through various forest disturbances including fires, pest infestation decay, or illegal harvesting. In accounting terms, the carbon credit received from the sequestration would be reversed in the future by debits in the account following disturbances such as decay and fires (Cairns and Lasserre 2006). If the forests are replanted or naturally regenerate at the same level of the decay and fire, the debits from decay and fire will be again offset as the carbon is once more sequestered. This cycle leads to the question of how can forests be managed to have a net gain in carbon sequestration? The possibilities include increasing the biomass (replanting and afforestation), reducing the release of carbon by forest fires and decay through forest management practices, and manufacturing harvested wood into wood products and replanting after the harvest.

The concept of assigning carbon sequestration offset credit for harvested wood products is currently being debated. Von Hagen and Burnett (2006) categorized forestry offsets into two categories: land management-based offsets and product-based offsets. Land management-based offsets are those offsets that increase the sequestration of carbon in forests, whereas product substitution-based offsets are those that potentially serve as offsets through the substitution of forest products for fuels, mostly fossil based, that have a greater carbon footprint. The land management-based offsets include:

- Forest conservation—Offsets that prevent deforestation.
- Afforestation—Offsets that plant trees on land that has not been forested previously.
- Reforestation—Offsets that plant trees in areas that have been harvested.
- Forest management—Offsets that aim to increase the biomass of the forest through extended rotations, reducing fire risk through forest thinning, and other forest stewardship practices.

Once forests are harvested, the carbon sequestration can continue if the harvested trees are manufactured into wood products. Sequestration stops when the wood products are burned or decay. Based on 2005 data, it was estimated that standing forests and harvested wood products sequester about 744 Tg of CO_2e annually (Skog 2008). The method of accounting for carbon sequestration from plantation through harvested wood products is called life cycle analysis (LCA). The LCA approach goes beyond the sequestration of carbon in natural forests and includes the carbon stored in harvested wood products and the substitution of energy-intensive building products, such as steel and concrete, by wood products (Perez-Garcia et al. 2005). Under the LCA approach, long cycles restrict return of carbon to the atmosphere. The second category of the von Hagen and Burnett (2006) classification of offsets accounts for product-based offsets and can be divided into the following three subcategories:

- Harvested wood products—Offsets that account for the carbon being sequestered in manufactured wood products.
- Material substitution—Offsets that account for the substitution effect of utilizing wood building products in place of other building products that are nonrenewable and do not sequester carbon. In addition to the sequestration within the wood products, carbon emissions are avoided by using a less emission-intensive manufacturing process.
- Energy substitution—Offsets that account for using forest biomass energy as a replacement for fossil fuels.

Note that inclusion of these three offset categories differs widely depending on the offset trading mechanism. The Kerry-Lieberman American Power Act allows offsets from harvested wood products and considers forest biomass energy carbon neutral, but it does not include material substitution offsets. The Copenhagen Climate Change Conference did address harvested wood product offsets with respect to reporting requirements and examining various approaches to retaining options. Specifically, progress was made in three areas (Bowyer et al. 2010). First, a resolution was drafted that harvested wood products in landfills will not receive offset credits. Second, the parties agreed to consider various alternatives to account for offsets from harvested wood products. Third, there were efforts made to begin drafting specific reporting requirements for countries. In spite of this general framework, there still is no final agreement on whether or not to include sequestration of carbon within harvested wood products in future climate change protocols.

Kyoto Protocol Offset System

The Kyoto Protocol framework was developed by the UNFCCC and serves as a global standard for emission allocation and offset systems. Although many countries did not participate in this agreement, the framework itself serves as a model for new agreements that are currently being negotiated. Therefore, it is important to understand the components of the Kyoto Protocol offset mechanism including the parties involved, compliance verification of funding sources, and the life cycle of an offset project. The offset mechanism developed by the Kyoto Protocol is the Clean Development Mechanism (CDM). Under this system, projects are developed to remove or reduce emissions, Certified Emission Reduction (CER) credits are issued, and these credits are sold through the European Climate Exchange. There are four main parties involved in the implementation of a carbon offset project (Kollmuss et al. 2008):

- Project owner—This is the entity that owns the physical installation where the project occurs. There are various categories of project owners including individuals, businesses, and nonprofit organizations.
- Project developer—This is the person or organization that is responsible to develop the emission reduction project. This developer could be the same as the project owner or an outside entity such as a consulting firm.
- Project funder—One of the key components of a project is the funding source. Funding could be in the form of loans or equity investments, and sources include individual investors, banks, private equity firms, nonprofits, and other organizations.
- Stakeholder—Stakeholders are parties that are affected directly or indirectly by the offset project. The various stakeholder groups include but are not limited to the project owner, developer, funder, local communities, nonprofit groups, national governments, and international agreements. Note that the interests of the various stakeholders differ and may not always be in agreement. For example, generally, the goal of project funders, owners, and developers is to maximize their return on investment and repatriate profits to their home country. In contrast, the goal of the host country is to develop their local communities where the project takes place and to retain investments within the local economy. Balancing the interests of the various stakeholders is a key to the success of any CDM project.

From implementation to completion there are many steps in a CDM project. The process starts with the development of an offset project concept and ends with the final project certification and commercialization. The CDM project life cycle was summarized by Kollmuss et al. (2008) and includes the following components:

- Project concept—This is a feasibility study that includes the technical feasibility, investment requirements, development and operational costs, expected returns, and other factors regarding the potential of the CDM project.
- Methodology—This defines the rules that the project developer must follow in order to calculate emission reductions. These include baseline and additionality requirements and the method to monitor the actual emissions reductions.

- Project design document—This documents the details of the CDM project and is used for all future planning and administrative procedures. The document outlines the exact methodology used to establish the baseline and to assure the additionality requirement. The general purpose of this document is to provide a record of how actual emission reductions will be realized from the project.

- Stakeholder consultations—All CDM projects are required to provide evidence that local populations and other stakeholders will not be adversely affected by the project. The project developer is required to inform stakeholders of the project through various forms of media, respond to all stakeholder comments, and describe a course of action to minimize negative impacts of the project.

- Project validation—This is a review process of the project that is conducted by an independent approved third party auditor defined as "designated operational entities" under CDM. This review process includes a review of the project design document, visits with project stakeholders, public comment period, resolution of stakeholder issues, and issuance of a final validation report. The final step of project validation is the submittal of this report along with the project design document to the CDM Executive Board for review and registration.

- Host country approval—Before final approval by the CDM Executive Board, the project must be approved by the host country. The project plan is checked against the host country's rules, regulations, laws, and sustainability criteria.

- Project registration—The CDM Executive Board conducts a final review of the project design document, validation report, public feedback, and the host country approval and, if all the CDM project criteria are met, the CDM Executive Board certifies the submitted project proposal as an official CDM project.

- Project implementation—Once the project receives approval from the CDM Executive Board, the project developers can start the project implementation. The project can also be implemented before the project receives final approval. However, the CDM Executive Board requires documentary evidence showing that the project meets CDM project criteria. If proper evidence is not supplied and the project is started, the project runs the risk of not receiving approval for reasons such as not meeting the additionality requirement.

- Project monitoring—All CDM project developers are required to maintain records and submit reports documenting the actual emission reductions that are being achieved by the project. The procedures for reporting are outlined in the original project design documents. There are no official requirements for how often these reports must be submitted. However, in order to receive revenue from achieved emission reductions, the project needs to generate CER credits, and these credits are issued against emission reduction reports. Therefore, the more frequently the reports are submitted, the more frequently revenue can be generated for the achieved emission reductions.
- Project verification—This is a periodic and independent review to verify that the emission reductions have occurred as reported by the project monitoring program. The auditors for the verification must be different from the project validation auditors in order to avoid conflict of interest.
- Project certification—Certification is the written assurance by the CDM Executive Board that the project has achieved a specified amount of emission reductions during a specified period.

The Kyoto Protocol stipulates that forests can be used for carbon sequestration to offset GHG emissions by signatory countries (Amano and Sedjo 2006). There are approximately 2,080 registered projects under CDM, ranging from clean energy development to agricultural projects (UNFCCC 2010). As of this writing in March 2010, there are only about 15 forestry-based projects (see appendix). It is important to understand the Kyoto Protocol standards for offset projects because it sets the standard for other offset mechanisms. Forest stakeholders in Alaska and other states can use the Kyoto Protocol standards as a template to understand the role of parties involved in offset projects and concepts such as baseline, additionality, verification, and certification.

Climate Change Legislation and Regional Agreements in the United States

There are three levels of climate change policy in the United States: federal, regional, and state. As of this writing, the only mandatory cap and trade program in the United States is the Regional Greenhouse Gas Initiative. This section gives a brief overview of the American Clean Energy Act and some of the regional and state GHG reduction schemes.

Climate Change Legislation

The United States is starting to formulate its own climate change mitigation policy. Two bills are currently under consideration. The first is the American Clean Energy and Security Act of 2009, also known as the Waxman-Markey Bill. This bill passed the U.S. Congress in June 2009 and was sent to the Senate. The primary goal of the bill is to reduce GHG emissions to 20 percent below 2005 levels by 2020 (Pew Center on Global Climate Change 2009). The second is the American Power Act, also known as the Kerry-Lieberman Bill in the Senate. The Kerry-Lieberman Bill calls for a 17-percent reduction below 2005 levels by 2020 (Pew Center on Global Climate Change 2009).

One key part of both bills is GHG emission offsets. In contrast to actual emission reductions, offsets sometimes are not permanent and may be reversible. For example, there may be an afforestation project that is modeled to sequester 1 MMTS of carbon for 80 years. However, there is the risk that the carbon may be re-released into the atmosphere earlier than outlined in the project description owing to forest fires or premature decay from pest infestation or disease. Thus, climate change mitigation strategies generally include a constraint on the quantity of offsets in order to ensure that actual emission reductions occur within the capped sector. Both bills address this issue by limiting offsets for covered entities to a maximum of 2 billion metric tons of their annual emissions through projects that reduce emissions outside the scope of the cap. The Waxman-Markey Bill also specifies that entities choosing to offset their emissions through emission reduction projects must reduce 1.25 metric tons of emissions through these projects (outside the cap) for every 1 metric ton of emissions they aim to offset from their operations. In other words, the quantity of the emissions reduction offset is slightly higher than the amount of emissions itself. For example, a coal powerplant desiring to offset 1 metric ton of CO_2 emissions could invest in an afforestation project deemed to sequester 1.25 metric tons of CO_2. A study by the EPA found that the offset program included in the bill would increase domestic afforestation efforts and methane capture from animal waste, and improve forest management activities and other carbon sequestration projects (EPA 2009b).

In addition to federal legislation, there are also regional agreements being formed to reduce GHGs. Three of the most prominent of these are the Western Climate Initiative (WCI), the Regional Greenhouse Gas Initiative (RGGI), and the Midwestern Greenhouse Gas Reduction Accord.

Western Climate Initiative

The WCI is a group of western states and provinces that have formed a regional coalition to combat climate change. The goal of the WCI is to reduce GHG emissions to 15 percent below 2005 levels by 2020, while maintaining economic growth. This coalition consists of seven U.S. states: Arizona, California, Montana, New Mexico, Oregon, Utah, and Washington. It also consists of four Canadian provinces: British Columbia, Quebec, Ontario, and Manitoba. Although Alaska is not actively participating in the WCI, the state is an observing member and may participate before the implementation. The initial framework for the WCI was released on September 23, 2008, and is scheduled to be fully implemented in 2015. This agreement will cover approximately 90 percent of the GHG emissions in WCI states and provinces and also allow offsets.

Regional Greenhouse Gas Initiative

The RGGI is a group of 10 Northeastern and Mid-Atlantic states: Connecticut, Delaware, Maine, Maryland, Massachusetts, New Hampshire, New Jersey, New York, Rhode Island, and Vermont (RGGI 2010). This is the first mandatory cap and trade GHG emissions reduction program in the United States. This agreement has set a target of reducing GHG emissions from the power sector 10 percent below 2009 levels by 2018. Emission allowances are auctioned off quarterly. In contrast to the WCI, which has yet to be implemented, the RGGI is now mandated and auctioning off emission permits as a tool to meet emission reduction targets. The RGGI invests funds collected from the auctions into energy efficiency and renewable energy programs. The RGGI allows offsets in five categories:

- Landfill methane capture and destruction.
- Reduction in emissions of sulphur hexafluoride in the electric power sector.
- Sequestration of carbon owing to afforestation.
- Reduction or avoidance of CO_2 emissions from natural gas, oil, or propane and end-use combustion owing to end-use energy efficiency in the building sector.
- Avoided methane emissions from agricultural manure management operations.

The systems developed by the RGGI and WCI are serving as frameworks for a national GHG reduction strategy. If a U.S. climate change bill does get signed into law, the members of RGGI and WCI will have a head start to adjusting to a potential cap and trade scheme initiated by that legislation.

The Midwestern Greenhouse Gas Reduction Accord

The Midwestern Greenhouse Gas Reduction Accord was established in 2007 and includes six states and one Canadian province. The members are Iowa, Illinois, Kansas, Michigan, Minnesota, Wisconsin, and Manitoba. It also encompasses four observer states that are included in the process but are not held to the mandated GHG reductions. These are Indiana, Ohio, Ontario, and South Dakota. This agreement establishes a cap and trade program with the goal of reducing GHG levels 20 percent below 2005 levels by December 31, 2020, and 80 percent below 2005 levels by December 31, 2050. The accord also includes an offset program and the monitoring and compliance mechanism to validate the offsets.

Carbon Exchanges

A majority of carbon offsets are currently traded on various exchanges, which are outlined below. As outlined above, the RGGI trades CO_2e allowances through its own in-house auctions, rather than offering these through climate exchanges.

The European Climate Exchange (ECX) is the largest climate exchange as measured by trading volumes (table 8). This exchange was established in 2005 and traded approximately US$125 billion worth of carbon credits in 2008 (ECX 2010a). The ECX is a clearing house for carbon allowance permits that are issued in line with Kyoto Protocol reduction requirements. The ECX uses a trading framework established under the European Union Emissions Trading Scheme, and two carbon products are traded. The first is the European allowance unit (EAU), which is equal to 1 metric ton of CO_2e emission allowance. The second is a CER. In contrast to an EAU, which is an allowance of emissions, a CER is a removal or avoidance of emissions. One CER represents a reduction or offset of GHG emissions of 1 metric ton of CO_2e. The Kyoto Protocol limits offsets to 5 percent of a country's assigned emission allowances.

Table 8—Volume of carbon dioxide equivalent (CO_2e) allowances traded

Year	European Climate Exchange	Chicago Climate Exchange	Regional Greenhouse Gas Initiative
	Million metric tons of CO_2e		
2005	321	1	N/A
2006	1101	10	N/A
2007	2060	23	N/A
2008	3093	72	65
2009	6326	62	805

N/A = not available.
Source: Capoor and Ambrosi 2009.

The primary carbon exchange in the United States is the Chicago Climate Exchange (CCX). Although the United States currently has no mandated GHG emission cap and trade system, CCX members make voluntary, but legally binding, commitments to reduce emissions that are verified by independent third party auditors. The CCX has recently initiated offset trading through their Carbon Financial Instrument®. These are contracts that cover projects involving the sequestration, destruction, or reduction of GHG emissions (CCX 2010). Other smaller exchanges include the Montreal Climate Exchange, the New South Wales Climate Exchange, and the Tianjin Climate Exchange.

The price of one EAU of CO_2e on the ECX has declined from about €28.50 in mid-2008 to €13.00 in April 2010 (ECX 2010b). This decline can be attributed to a number of factors including the supply of carbon allowances, the economic slowdown, and the uncertainty of what framework will govern CO_2e allowances post 2012. The decline has been more drastic in the voluntary market, where prices have declined from a mid-2008 price of about US$7.00 to a price of US$0.10 in April 2010. Price comparisons between the CCX and ECX illustrate how a mandated emission reduction system leads to a higher price (fig. 3).

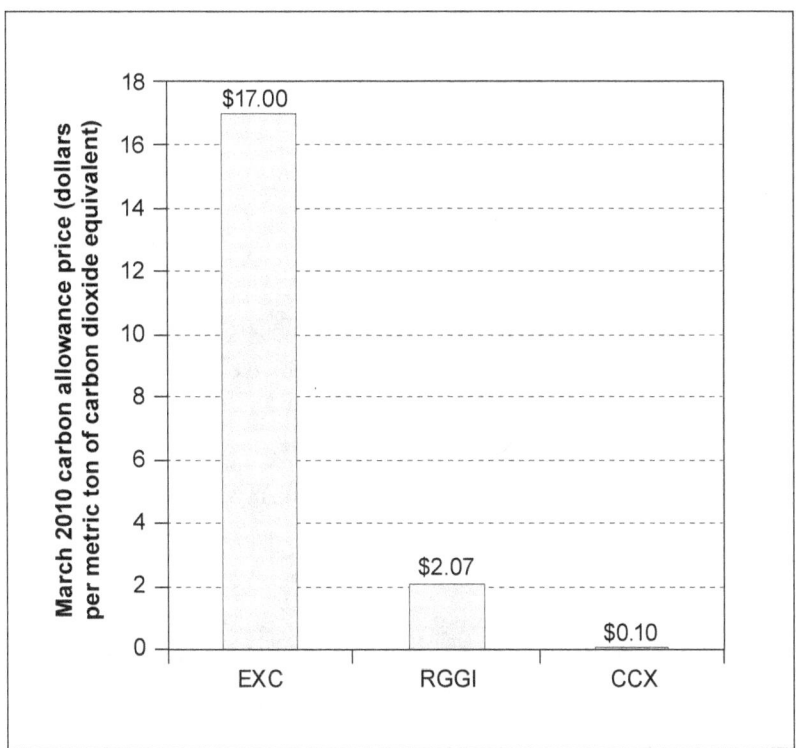

Figure 3—March 2010 carbon allowance pricing. Note: EXC = European Climate Exchange, RGGI = Regional Greenhouse Gas Initiative, CCX = Chicago Climate Exchange. Sources: CCX 2010, EXC 2010b, RGGI 2010.

The above are large-scale frameworks for reducing GHG emissions. However, there is also demand from individuals and businesses that wish to reduce GHGs but do not have the scale to participate in the larger exchanges. Therefore, a number of entities have emerged to supply offsets on a smaller scale to individuals and businesses (table 9). There are three key ingredients maintaining a viable offset market. First, there must be a supply and demand for the offsets. Second, there must be a market to buy and sell the offsets. Third, there must be a third party organization to independently verify the offset project. An example of a smaller scale offset project generated by an independent agency is the Genesis Forest Project funded by Carbonfund.org (Carbonfund.org 2009). The goal of this project is to protect about 1215 hectares (3,000 acres) of tropical forest land, which Carbonfund.org estimates will sequester approximately 90,000 metric tons of CO_2. These offsets can then be sold to individuals or businesses by Carbonfund.org directly.

Table 9—Small-scale offset mechanisms

Carbon offset organization	Project type	Independent certification/verification entity
Versus Carbon Neutral	Various	Chicago Climate Exchange (CCX)
E-Blue Horizons	Renewable energy, reforestation	CCX, Environmental Resources Trust (ERT)
Carbonfund.org	Renewable energy, energy efficiency, reforestation	ERT, Climate Community and Biodiversity Standards, CCX, Kyoto Protocol Joint Implementation
Liveneutral.org	Energy efficiency	CCX

Conclusions

Forests cover 52.3 million hectares (129 million acres) of Alaska or about one-third of the state. Forest lands in Alaska are owned by the federal government (65 percent), the state of Alaska (24.5 percent), regional and native corporations (10 percent), and 0.5 percent by other private interests (State of Alaska 2010). Alaskan forests are a major carbon sink, accounting for approximately 17 percent of all U.S. forest land. A GHG offset mechanism would provide an incentive to manage Alaskan forests to maximize carbon sequestration. This would include afforestation, reforestation, and reduced deforestation. This could become a revenue stream for stakeholders that control timberland including Alaska's native corporations, private landowners, the state of Alaska, and possibly the federal government. However, it is important to understand that Alaska timberland owners would also face high operating costs and relatively slow growth rates for afforestation and reforestation projects. Therefore, the price of carbon offsets would have to be at a level to offset the operating costs and provide a reasonable return on investment.

In addition to afforestation, reforestation, and reduced deforestation, the Kerry-Lieberman Bill addresses harvested wood products. In its current form, the bill states that forest management activities that result in "an increase in forest carbon stores, including harvested wood products" would qualify as offsets (Pew Center on Climate Change 2010). The incentive for Alaskan forest landowners under this scenario would be to harvest timber, manufacture wood products, and replant the timber. This is due to the additional offset credits that are offered for extending the carbon sequestration period by continuing to sequester the carbon within the wood products. Because the wood supply from federal timberland is constricted, this would have the largest impact on state and native corporation timberlands.

The future of a cap and trade system in the United States is uncertain. As of this writing July 2010, the Senate is trying to gather the 60 votes required for the passage of a climate change bill. One key factor that will impact the passage of a climate change bill is the November 2010 mid-term elections. If a cap and trade bill does not pass, the United States can still pursue GHG emission reductions through regional agreements such as the WCI, RGGI, and the Midwestern Greenhouse Gas Reduction Accord. Forest-based offsets will play an important role in these regional agreements. Another pending issue is what global climate change agreement will follow the Kyoto Protocol and to what extent will the United States participate? Without a climate change bill, the one tool left to the administration to negotiate a global climate change agreement is regulating emissions through the EPA. In conclusion, emission reductions are a global priority, and it can be expected that the United States will play a role in these efforts.

Acknowledgments

This report is based upon work supported by the U.S Forest Service, University of Washington, University of Alaska, and Cooperative State Research, Education and Extension Service, U.S. Department of Agriculture, under Agreement No. 2008-34158-19474. Any opinions, findings, conclusions, or recommendations expressed in this publication are those of the author(s) and do not necessarily reflect the view of the U.S. Department of Agriculture.

English Equivalents

When you know:	Multiply by:	To find:
Hectares	2.47	Acres
Metric tons or tonnes	1.102	Tons or short tons
Teragrams (Tg)	1.101×10^6	Tons

References

Amano, M.; Sedjo, R.A. 2006. Forest sequestration: performance in selected countries in the Kyoto period and the potential role of sequestration in post-Kyoto agreements. Washington, DC: Resources for the Future. 59 p.

Bowyer, J.; Bratkovich, S.; Howe, J.; Fernholz, K. 2010. Recognition of carbon storage in harvested wood products: a post-Copenhagen update. Minneapolis, MN: Dovetail Partners, Inc. 20 p.

Brown, S. 2002. Report of leakage analysis for the Noel Kempff averted deforestation component: land use and forest, carbon monitoring, and global change. Arlington, VA: Winrock International and Ecosecurities Ltd. 16 p.

Cairns, R.D.; Lasserre, P. 2006. Implementing carbon credits for forests based on green accounting. Ecological Economics. 56(4): 610–621.

Capoor, K.; Ambrosi, P. 2007. State and trends of the carbon market 2007. Washington, DC: The World Bank. 45 p.

Carbonfund.org. 2009. Reforestation and avoided deforestation projects. http://www.carbonfund.org/site/projects/reforestation. (April 2010).

Center for Climate Strategies. 2009. Final Alaska greenhouse gas inventory and reference case projections, 1990–2025. 92 p. http://www.akclimatechange.us/ewebeditpro/items/O97F21897.pdf. (April 2010).

Chicago Climate Exchange [CCX]. 2010. CCX offset program. http://www.chicagoclimatex.com/content.jsf?id=23. (02 April 2010).

Climate Action Reserve [CAR]. 2009. Forest project protocol-version 3.0. Los Angeles, CA. 105 p. http://www.climateactionreserve.org/wp-content/uploads/2009/03/Forest-Project-Protocol-Version-3.0.pdf. (04 May 2010).

Energy Information Administration [EIA]. 2009. International energy outlook 2009. DOE/EIA-0484(2009). Washington, DC: U.S. Department of Energy. 274 p.

Environmental Protection Agency [EPA]. 2009a. EPA: greenhouse gases threaten public health and the environment/science overwhelmingly shows greenhouse gas concentrations at unprecedented levels due to human activity. News Release. 07 December. http://yosemite.epa.gov/opa/admpress.nsf/d985312f6895893b852574ac005f1e40/08d11a451131bca585257685005bf252!OpenDocument. (April 2010).

Environmental Protection Agency [EPA]. 2009b. EPA preliminary analysis of the Waxman-Markey discussion draft: The American Clean Energy and Security Act of 2009 in the 111th Congress. http://www.epa.gov/climatechange/economics/pdfs/WM-Analysis.pdf. (April 2010).

Environmental Protection Agency [EPA]. 2009c. Inventory of U.S. greenhouse gas emissions and sinks: 1990–2007. EPA 430-R-09-004. Washington, DC. 440 p.

European Climate Exchange [ECX]. 2010a. About ECX. http://www.ecx.eu/About-ECX. (25 January 2010).

European Climate Exchange [ECX]. 2010b. ECX products. http://www.ecx.eu/ECX-Products. (9 March 2010).

International Emissions Trading Association [IETA]. 2009. What are carbon dioxide equivalents (CO_2 eq)? http://www.ieta.org/ieta/www/pages/index.php?IdSitePage=123. (11 December 2010).

Kollmuss, A.; Zink, H.; Polycarp, C. 2008. Making sense of the voluntary carbon market: a comparison of carbon offset standards. 105 p. http://assets.panda.org/downloads/vcm_report_final.pdf. (April 2010).

Offset Quality Initiative. 2008. About offsets. http://www.offsetqualityinitiative.org/offsets.html. (April 2010).

Perez-Garcia, J.; Lippke, B. 2008. How can certain forest lands and products participate as an offset or other credit in a cap and trade program? Washington State Department of Ecology, contract No. C0800361. 6/30: 3–5. On file with: Joseph Roos.

Perez-Garcia, J.; Lippke, B.; Comnick, J.; Manriquez, C. 2005. An assessment of carbon pools, storage, and wood products market substitution using life-cycle analysis results. Wood and Fiber Science. 37: 140–148.

Pew Center on Global Climate Change. 2009. Summary of the American Clean Energy and Security Act of 2009. http://www.pewclimate.org/docUploads/WaxmanMarkey%20summary_FINAL_7.31.pdf. (April 2010).

Pew Center on Global Climate Change. 2010. Summary of the American Power Act of 2010. http://www.pewclimate.org/docUploads/detailed-summary-kerry-lieberman.pdf. (April 2010).

Regional Greenhouse Gas Initiative [RGGI]. 2010. Welcome. http://www.rggi.org. (1 April 2010).

Santilli, M.; Moutinho, P.; Schwartzman, S.; Nepstad, D.; Curran, L.; Nobre, C. 2005. Tropical deforestation and the Kyoto Protocol: an editorial essay. Climatic Change. 71: 267–276.

Skog, K.E. 2008. Sequestration of carbon in harvested wood products for the United States. Forest Products Journal. 58(6): 56–72.

State of Alaska. 2010. Sources of timber supply. http://www.commerce.state.ak.us/oed/forest_products/forest_products2.htm. (July 2010).

United Nations Framework Convention on Climate Change [UNFCCC]. 2009. Copenhagen Accord draft. 6 p. http://unfccc.int/files/meetings/cop_15/application/pdf/cop15_cph_auv.pdf. (April 2010).

United Nations Framework Convention on Climate Change [UNFCCC]. 2010. CDM statistics. http://cdm.unfccc.int/Statistics/index.html. (10 March 2010).

United Nations Statistics Division. 2009. Environmental indicators: GHGs. http://unstats.un.org/unsd/ENVIRONMENT/air_greenhouse_emissions.htm. (7 April 2010).

U.S. Census Bureau. 2010. Population. http://www.census.gov/compendia/statab/cats/population.html. (25 February 2010).

von Hagen, B.; Burnett, M. 2006. Emerging markets for carbon stored by Northwest forests. In: Forests, carbon and climate change: a synthesis of science findings. Portland, OR: Oregon Forest Resources Institute: 131–155.

Western Climate Initiative [WCI]. 2009. Offset definition (task 1.1) and eligibility criteria (task 1.2) white paper. Offsets Committee document. July 24. http://www.westernclimateinitiative.org/component/remository/Offsets-Committee-Documents/. (April 2010).

Glossary

Carbon dioxide equivalent (CO₂e)—The universal unit of measurement used to indicate the global warming potential of each of the six greenhouse gases regulated under the Kyoto Protocol.

Certified emission reductions (CERs)—A unit of greenhouse gas emission reductions issued pursuant to the Clean Development Mechanism of the Kyoto Protocol, and measured in metric tons of carbon dioxide equivalent. One CER represents a reduction in greenhouse gas emissions of 1 metric ton of CO_2e.

Clean development mechanism (CDM)—The mechanism provided by Article 12 of the Kyoto Protocol, designed to assist developing countries in achieving sustainable development by allowing entities from Annex I Parties (industrial countries) to participate.

Emission reduction units (ERUs)—A unit of emission reductions issued pursuant to Joint Implementation. One ERU represents the right to emit 1 metric ton of carbon dioxide equivalent.

Global warming potential (GWP)—A measure of how much a given mass of greenhouse gas is estimated to contribute to global warming. It is a relative scale that compares the gas in question to that of the same mass of carbon dioxide (whose GWP is by convention equal to 1). A GWP is calculated over a specific time interval and this time interval must be stated whenever a GWP is quoted or else the value is meaningless.

Greenhouse gases (GHGs)—Both natural and anthropogenic, GHGs trap heat in the Earth's atmosphere, causing the greenhouse effect.

Kyoto Protocol—An international agreement linked to the United Nations Framework Convention on Climate Change. The major feature of the Kyoto Protocol is that it sets binding targets for 37 industrialized countries and the European community for reducing greenhouse gas emissions. This amounts to an average of 5 percent against 1990 levels over the 5-year period 2008–2012.

Joint implementation (JI)—Mechanism provided by Article 6 of the Kyoto Protocol whereby entities from Annex I Parties (industrialized countries as defined by the Kyoto Protocol) may participate in low-carbon projects hosted in Annex I countries and obtain emission reduction units in return.

United Nations Framework Convention on Climate Change (UNFCCC)—The international legal framework adopted in June 1992 at the Rio Earth Summit to address climate change. It commits the parties to the UNFCCC to stabilize human-induced greenhouse gas emissions at levels that would prevent dangerous manmade interference with the climate system, following "common but differentiated responsibilities" based on "respective capabilities."

Appendix: Examples of Kyoto Protocol Clean Development Mechanism (CDM) Offset Projects

Date registered	Title	Host parties	Other parties	Reductions
				Million metric tons CO₂e
11/10/06	Facilitating Reforestation for Guangxi Watershed Management in Pearl River Basin	China	Italy, Spain	25 795
1/30/09	Moldova Soil Conservation Project	Republic of Moldova	Sweden, Netherlands	179 242
3/23/09	Small-Scale Cooperative Afforestation CDM Pilot Project Activity on Private Lands Affected by Shifting Sand Dunes in Sirsa, Haryana	India	N/A	11 596
4/28/09	Cao Phong Reforestation Project	Viet Nam	N/A	2665
6/5/09	Reforestation of Severely Degraded Landmass in Khammam District of Andhra Pradesh, India under ITC Social Forestry Project	India	N/A	57 792
6/11/09	Carbon Sequestration Through Reforestation in the Bolivian Tropics by Smallholders of "The Federación de Comunidades Agro-pecuarias de Rurrenabaque (FECAR)"	Bolivia	Belgium	4341
8/21/09	Uganda Nile Basin Reforestation Project No. 3	Uganda	Italy	5564
9/6/09	Reforestation of Croplands and Grasslands in Low Income Communities of Paraguarí Department, Paraguay	Paraguay	Japan	1523
Under review	Reforestation as Renewable Source of Wood Supplies for Industrial Use in Brazil	Brazil	Netherlands	75 783
11/16/09	Afforestation and Reforestation on Degraded Lands in Northwest Sichuan, China	China	N/A	23 030
11/16/09	Reforestation, sustainable production and carbon sequestration project in José Ignacio Távara's dry forest, Piura, Peru	Peru	N/A	48 689
12/7/09	Humbo Ethiopia Assisted Natural Regeneration Project	Ethiopia	Canada	29 343
1/2/10	Assisted Natural Regeneration of Degraded Lands in Albania	Albania	Italy	22 964
1/15/10	The International Small Group and Tree Planting Program (TIST), Tamil Nadu, India	India	U.K. and Northern Ireland	3594
Requesting registration	Forestry Project for the Basin of the Chinchiná River, an Environmental and Productive Alternative for the City and the Region	Colombia	N/A	37 783

N/A = not applicable; CO₂e = carbon dioxide equivalents.
Source: UNFCCC 2010.